July 2012

OVERSEAS RIGHTSIZING

State Has Improved the Consistency of Its Approach, but Does Not Follow Up on Its Recommendations

GAO

Accountability ★ Integrity ★ Reliability

GAO-12-799

GAO
Accountability * Integrity * Reliability

Highlights

Highlights of GAO-12-799, a report to the Committee on Foreign Relations, U.S. Senate

OVERSEAS RIGHTSIZING

State Has Improved the Consistency of Its Approach, but Does Not Follow Up on Its Recommendations

Why GAO Did This Study

After the 1998 bombings of two U.S. embassies, a U.S. government panel determined that staffing levels had not been adjusted to reflect changing missions, requirements, and security concerns. In 2004, Congress mandated the establishment of the Office of Rightsizing within the Department of State. The office reviews levels of overseas staffing for all U.S. government agencies at every post every 5 years, projects future staffing levels it determines are appropriate to meet mission needs, and recommends ways to improve efficiency. Rightsizing is intended to align the number and location of staff with foreign policy priorities, security, and other constraints.

GAO examined (1) the consistency of State's approach to conducting rightsizing reviews and how its projections compare to actual staffing levels; (2) the focus of State's rightsizing recommendations; and (3) the extent to which State uses its rightsizing reviews and monitors implementation of recommendations. GAO reviewed 181 rightsizing reviews, compared projections in reviews with current actual staffing data, and interviewed officials from State and other agencies in Washington, D.C., and at overseas posts.

What GAO Recommends

GAO recommends that the Secretary of State designate the appropriate entities to ensure that rightsizing recommendations are addressed and to track and report the actions taken to implement the recommendations. State described a number of actions it intends to take that could address GAO's recommendations.

View GAO-12-799. For more information, contact Michael J. Courts at (202) 512-8980 or courtsm@gao.gov.

What GAO Found

The Department of State (State) has improved the consistency of its rightsizing approach across overseas posts. However, differences between future staffing levels it projects are appropriate to meet mission needs and actual staffing levels still exist due to unanticipated events and other factors. GAO reported in 2006 that State's Office of Management Policy, Rightsizing and Innovation (M/PRI) had not been conducting its rightsizing reviews consistently. Some reviews discussed various rightsizing elements, such as outsourcing, while others did not. State has since improved the consistency of its reviews by developing a variety of methodological tools and a standard template which it applies to each post. GAO found that over half of the 144 rightsizing projections analyzed were within 10 percent of actual staffing levels as of December 2011. In contrast, over 40 percent of the posts have staffing level differences of over 10 percent. Unanticipated events and other factors, such as changes in policies, contributed to these differences. For example, according to the management officer in Mozambique, M/PRI projected staffing increases as a result of the President's program to combat AIDS, but the actual funding level for the program was much higher than anticipated. This resulted in higher actual staffing levels for both U.S. direct-hire and locally-employed staff positions.

Rightsizing reviews contain recommendations to improve post operations and eliminate duplicative services and positions. To develop its recommendations, M/PRI reviews the levels of all staff at posts and seeks input from State and non-State agencies. M/PRI relies on non-State agencies to determine independently their own staffing needs. Many of State's recommendations for a specific post focus on the level of State's administrative or management staff, rather than State's programmatic staff or staff from other agencies. Some State officials stated that the activities of administrative and management staff are better suited to quantitative measurement while the qualitative nature of programmatic staff activities, such as discussing policy issues with foreign diplomatic counterparts, is more difficult to measure.

State's use of rightsizing reviews varies, and State does not follow up on review recommendations. State's Bureau of Overseas Buildings Operations uses the staffing projections in rightsizing reviews to plan the size of new embassy compounds. Further, M/PRI uses rightsizing reviews when it assesses requests by State or other agencies to add staff to overseas posts, although the final decision is made by the respective Chief of Mission. In addition, Bureau of Diplomatic Security officials said that they incorporate rightsizing reviews into their annual staffing planning exercise, and some post officials said that they refer to rightsizing reviews to support staffing changes. Some U.S. officials stated that undertaking the rightsizing process acts as a check on growth in overseas staffing levels. However, some State regional bureau officials said that they do not actively use the reviews except as a historical overview of staffing, and some post officials said that they do not use the reviews at all. State often uses documents other than rightsizing reviews for decisions in areas including staffing levels. Finally, State does not monitor the implementation of rightsizing review recommendations and has not designated an office with responsibility for their implementation. State issues an annual report to Congress in which it lists the rightsizing reviews it has completed, number of positions recommended for elimination, and potential cost savings; the report does not address whether recommendations have been implemented. Because State does not track or report on the implementation of recommendations, State cannot determine if rightsizing reviews are achieving their purpose of aligning overseas staffing levels with U.S. priorities.

_____ United States Government Accountability Office

Contents

Abbreviations

DOD	Department of Defense
ICASS	International Cooperative Administrative Support Services
M/PRI	Office of Management Policy, Rightsizing and Innovation
MSRP	Mission Strategic Resource Plan
NSDD-38	National Security Decision Directive 38
OBO	Bureau of Overseas Buildings Operations
OIG	Office of Inspector General
PEPFAR	President's Emergency Plan for AIDS Relief
State	Department of State
USAID	U.S. Agency for International Development

GAO
Accountability * Integrity * Reliability

United States Government Accountability Office
Washington, DC 20548

July 25, 2012

The Honorable John F. Kerry
Chairman
The Honorable Richard G. Lugar
Ranking Member
Committee on Foreign Relations
United States Senate

After the 1998 terrorist bombings of U.S. embassies in Dar es Salaam, Tanzania, and Nairobi, Kenya, a U.S. government panel convened to conduct an assessment of overseas presence determined that the staffing levels at embassies and consulates worldwide had not been adjusted to reflect changing missions, requirements, and security concerns. In 2004, Congress mandated the establishment of the Office of Rightsizing within the Department of State (State).[1] This office, now part of the Office of Management Policy, Rightsizing and Innovation (M/PRI), reviews staffing levels for all U.S. government agencies at every overseas mission[2] once every 5 years and before undertaking all capital construction projects. The office also projects future staffing levels that it determines are appropriate to meet the missions' needs and recommends ways to improve efficiency. Since 2002, we have conducted several reviews related to U.S. government staffing overseas.[3] In these reviews, we examined the rightsizing process and issues related to the construction of new facilities overseas, among other things. In 2006, we found that the information presented within rightsizing reviews varied from

---

[1]Pub. L. No. 108-199, Div. B, Title IV; 118 Stat. 80.

[2]U.S. overseas missions can encompass multiple locations, or posts, within a country. For example, the U.S. mission to Germany comprises six posts, including an embassy in Berlin, and consulates in Dusseldorf, Frankfurt, Hamburg, Leipzig, and Munich.

[3]See GAO, *Overseas Presence: Framework for Assessing Embassy Staff Levels Can Support Rightsizing Initiatives*, GAO-02-780 (Washington, D.C.: Jul. 26, 2002); GAO, *Embassy Construction: Process for Determining Staffing Requirements Needs Improvement*, GAO-03-411 (Washington, D.C.: Apr. 7, 2003); GAO, *Overseas Staffing: Rightsizing Approaches Slowly Taking Hold but More Action Needed to Coordinate and Carry Out Efforts*, GAO-06-737 (Washington, D.C.: Jun. 30, 2006); and GAO, *New Embassy Compounds: State Faces Challenges in Sizing Facilities and Providing for Operations and Maintenance Requirements*, GAO-10-689 (Washington, D.C.: Jul. 20, 2010).

GAO-12-799 Overseas Rightsizing

post to post, and the rightsizing elements that the posts evaluated and reported were not consistent.

In response to your request, we examined (1) the consistency of State's approach to conducting rightsizing reviews and how its projections compare to actual staffing levels; (2) the focus of State's rightsizing recommendations; and (3) the extent to which State uses its rightsizing reviews and monitors implementation of recommendations.

To address these objectives, we reviewed rightsizing guidance, related legislation, 181 rightsizing reviews State undertook from 2005 through 2011, and previous GAO reports related to U.S. government staffing levels overseas. We reviewed 14 rightsizing reviews in greater depth, to obtain additional information about the rightsizing process, the differences between projected and actual staffing levels, and post officials' use of the reviews. We conducted site visits at 3 of the posts: Prague, the Czech Republic; Sarajevo, Bosnia-Herzegovina; and Kuwait City, Kuwait. We communicated via teleconference and other means with the additional posts. To compare projected staffing levels in rightsizing reviews with actual staffing levels as of December 2011, we compared staffing data from State's personnel database as of December 2011 with the staffing projections of 144 rightsizing reviews State conducted from 2006 through 2011. We did not include all of the rightsizing reviews in the comparison between the actual and projected staffing levels for various methodological reasons, such as data reliability concerns and review time frames that were outside the scope of our analysis. To assess the reasons for the differences between the projection and the actual staffing levels, we constructed a composite index for each country taking into account the differences in staffing levels for various personnel categories. We then sent questions to the management officers in 10 countries with the highest indices: 5 for reviews that had projected staff levels that were higher than actual levels and 5 for those that had projected levels that were lower than actual levels. In addition, we discussed rightsizing with State officials in Washington, D.C., from M/PRI, State's regional bureaus, the Bureau of Overseas Buildings Operations (OBO), the Bureau of Diplomatic Security, and the Bureau of Consular Affairs. We also discussed rightsizing with officials from non-State agencies based in Washington, D.C. or overseas, including the Departments of Defense (DOD); Commerce; Health and Human Services; Homeland Security; and Justice; and the U.S. Agency for International Development (USAID). Appendix I provides more information on our scope and methodology.

We conducted this performance audit from July 2011 to July 2012 in accordance with generally accepted government auditing standards. Those standards require that we plan and perform the audit to obtain sufficient, appropriate evidence to provide a reasonable basis for our findings and conclusions based on our audit objectives. We believe that the evidence obtained provides a reasonable basis for our findings and conclusions based on our audit objectives.

Background

The U.S. government maintains more than 270 diplomatic posts, including embassies, consulates, and other diplomatic offices, in about 180 countries worldwide. More than 80,000 U.S. government employees work overseas, including both U.S. direct hires and locally-employed staff under chief of mission[4] authority, representing more than 30 agencies and government entities. Agencies represented overseas include the Departments of Agriculture, Commerce, Defense, Homeland Security, Justice, State, the Treasury, and USAID.

In the aftermath of the August 1998 bombings of two U.S. embassies in Africa, State formed the Overseas Presence Advisory Panel to conduct an assessment of overseas presence. The panel determined that overseas staffing levels had not been adjusted to reflect changing missions, requirements, and security concerns. Some missions were overstaffed, while others were understaffed. In 2002, we outlined a framework for assessing overseas staff levels.[5] In 2003, we found that U.S. agencies' staffing projections for new embassy compounds were developed without a systematic approach or comprehensive rightsizing analysis.[6]

In 2004, Congress mandated the establishment of the Office of Rightsizing within State. The Office of Rightsizing was combined with two other offices in 2007 to create M/PRI. The House Foreign Affairs

---

[4]A chief of mission is the principal officer, usually the Ambassador, in charge of a U.S. diplomatic mission abroad, and has full responsibility for the direction, coordination, and supervision of all U.S. government executive branch employees in that country (except for Voice of America correspondents on official assignment and employees under the command of a U.S. area military commander). See 22 U.S.C. 3927.

[5]GAO-02-780.

[6]GAO-03-411.

Committee directed the office to lead State's efforts to develop internal and interagency mechanisms to coordinate, rationalize, and manage the deployment of U.S. government staff overseas. This legislation was intended to result in the reallocation of resources to achieve a leaner, streamlined, more agile and secure U.S. government presence abroad. The conference report accompanying the legislation establishing the Office of Rightsizing stated that a proper rightsizing plan should include a systematic analysis to bring about a reconfiguration of overseas staffing to the number necessary to achieve U.S. foreign policy needs, and noted that rationalizing staffing and operations abroad had the potential for significant budgetary savings. The office was directed by the Senate Foreign Relations Committee to review all U.S. government staffing overseas, including all American and foreign national personnel, in all employment categories. The House Foreign Affairs Committee also directed OBO to work closely with M/PRI to ensure that projected staffing levels for new embassy compounds were prepared in a disciplined and realistic manner, and that these estimates become a basis for determining the size, configuration, and budget of new embassy construction projects.

M/PRI conducts rightsizing reviews before each construction project and on each mission every 5 years, among other responsibilities.[7] M/PRI focuses on streamlining staffing levels by, for example, consolidating or outsourcing administrative functions. M/PRI also looks for opportunities to substitute less expensive, locally-employed staff for more expensive U.S. direct-hire employees.[8] According to the guidance M/PRI provides to

---

[7]The legislation establishing the Office of Rightsizing also directed the Secretary of State to require chiefs of mission to review, not less than once every 5 years, every staff element under their authority, including staff from other departments or agencies of the United States, and recommend approval or disapproval of each staff element. Pub. L. No. 108-447, Div. B. sec. 409(a). M/PRI coordinates this process and provides analysis of chief of mission submissions.

[8]U.S. overseas missions are staffed by both U.S. direct-hire and locally-employed staff, all of whom are considered during the rightsizing process. U.S. direct-hire staff work directly for a U.S. government agency (i.e., are not contractors); individuals who are hired locally to work at U.S. missions overseas are referred to as locally-employed staff. U.S. direct-hire staff salaries are paid for by budgets in Washington, D.C., while locally-employed staff salaries and benefits are paid for out of a specific post's budget. M/PRI estimates that the average cost to maintain a U.S. direct-hire position overseas is approximately $530,000 annually, which includes housing and other benefits and allowances. Costs for locally-employed staff, who do not receive the same benefits and allowances as U.S. direct-hire staff, are often significantly less.

overseas missions, a rightsizing analysis may lead to the reallocation of resources from one mission goal to another and to enhancing operational efficiency through regionalization[9] and centralization. M/PRI uses GAO's definition of rightsizing: aligning the number and location of staff assigned overseas with foreign policy priorities, security concerns, and other constraints. Rightsizing may result in the addition or reduction of staff, or a change in the mix of staff at a given embassy or consulate. M/PRI's guidance stresses that all sections and agencies of an overseas mission should be included in a rightsizing analysis.

In the first step of the rightsizing process, overseas missions, generally led by the mission's management officer, prepare a report for M/PRI outlining their strategic goals, current staffing data for all agencies, and projected staffing levels 5 years into the future. State and non-State agencies present at an overseas mission provide their staffing data to be included in the mission's submission to M/PRI. M/PRI officials stated that, under their current process, an M/PRI analyst usually visits the mission to assist in preparing the rightsizing report. After a mission completes its rightsizing report, the relevant regional bureau approves the submission before sending it to M/PRI. Next, M/PRI conducts its analysis of staffing at the mission, coordinating with the headquarters of non-State agencies to confirm the numbers provided at the mission for those agencies. When M/PRI completes a draft rightsizing review, other State bureaus and agencies have the opportunity to review and discuss it. According to officials from State bureaus, they frequently engage in a dialogue with M/PRI to negotiate the staffing projections to be published in the rightsizing review and in a majority of cases, differences in projected staffing numbers are resolved through these discussions. Once all bureaus and agencies have reviewed the rightsizing review document, M/PRI finalizes and publishes it on an internal State website. Since its creation in 2004, State's rightsizing office has conducted 224 reviews.[10] According to M/PRI officials, all overseas missions have undergone the process once, and a second round of reviews is now under way.

---

[9]Regionalization could include outsourcing certain activities, such as voucher examining, from a post to a regional center or U.S. office.

[10] M/PRI provided us with 181 rightsizing reviews within the time frame of our analysis. Since that time, M/PRI has completed additional reviews.

The staffing levels of a mission are determined by the chief of mission through the National Security Decision Directive 38 (NSDD-38)[11] process, which provides authority for the chief of mission to determine the size, composition, or mandate of personnel operating at the mission. To add or abolish U.S. direct-hire positions at a mission, agencies electronically submit an NSDD-38 request for the chief of mission to either approve or deny. Requests may only include one agency in one country, but may include requests for multiple positions. Formal submission is generally preceded by informal discussions about the requested positions, according to officials.

State Has Improved the Consistency of Its Approach, but Unanticipated Events and Other Factors Contribute to Differences between Actual and Projected Staff Levels

State has improved the consistency of its analyses across overseas missions, but differences between actual and projected staffing levels still exist due to unanticipated events and other factors. We reported in 2006 that the Office of Management Policy, Rightsizing, and Innovation (M/PRI) had not been conducting its rightsizing reviews in a consistent manner.[12] State has since improved the consistency of its reviews by developing a variety of methodological tools and a standard template that it applies to each mission. These tools include ratios and formulas that compare missions similar in size and foreign policy priority to help M/PRI project what the office determines is the appropriate level of staffing at each mission. We found that although actual staffing levels as of December 2011 were within 10 percent of projected staffing levels in over half of the reviews we analyzed, over 40 percent of the missions have staffing level differences over 10 percent. Unanticipated events and other factors, such as changes in policies and priorities, contributed to the differences between actual and projected staffing levels.

---

[11]NSDD-38 states that agencies with staff under chief of mission authority will ensure that approval from the chief of mission is sought, in coordination with State, before making any proposed changes to the size, composition, or mandate of the agencies' staffing elements at the post.

[12] GAO-06-737.

State Has Improved the Consistency of Its Rightsizing Reviews Since 2006

With its current approach to rightsizing, State has improved the consistency of its analysis across overseas missions. In 2006, we reported that the information presented in rightsizing reviews varied from mission to mission and the rightsizing elements that missions evaluated and reported were not consistent.[13] Some missions provided narratives discussing various rightsizing elements, such as outsourcing and post security, while others did not. The reviews ranged in length from less than 5 pages to over 20 pages.

According to current M/PRI officials, the methodology used in the rightsizing process has evolved since the office was created. M/PRI officials stated that their reviews are now more standardized than in the past. The reviews now contain the same types of information in a similar format and have a more uniform level of detail. The required elements of a rightsizing review include detailed analysis of current and projected staff for each section of an overseas mission, as shown in table 1. M/PRI has also refined its methodology for analyzing administrative, management, and program staff. M/PRI has developed uniform guidance for staff at overseas missions to use in preparing rightsizing submissions. The majority of State officials at posts we visited that had participated in a rightsizing review said that the M/PRI guidance was helpful for the post in completing its submission.

---

[13] GAO-06-737.

Table 1: Summary of Required Elements of Rightsizing Reviews

Element	Description
Mission goals and objectives	For each mission goal, identify the resources currently supporting that goal, and analyze the post's specific achievements in meeting the objectives.
Current and projected staffing	Analyze current and projected staffing in each section of an overseas post and for each agency, using comparative indicators. Complete the summary staffing table, including all sections and/or agencies, showing current staffing levels, projected staffing levels, and the net change.
Duplicative activities	Assess areas of duplication, activities that are no longer required or may require adjustment of resource levels, and identify activities that require increased resources to achieve their objectives.
Competitive sourcing	Identify services that are or could be outsourced, including services contracted by the embassy such as local guard services, vehicle maintenance, janitor services, gardening services, etc.
Regionalized services	Identify activities that are or could be performed by regional or U.S.-based government personnel such as financial management and human resources services.
Substitution of locally-employed staff for U.S. direct-hire positions	Identify U.S. direct-hire or eligible family member positions for which locally-employed staff may be substituted.
ICASS[a] workload count	Compare the productivity of locally-employed staff in the different management service functions to worldwide average productivity and to the productivity of staff at other posts of approximately the same size and operating environment.

Source: GAO and M/PRI.

[a]The International Cooperative Administrative Support Services (ICASS) system provides more than 30 services—including financial management, human resources, and travel services, among others—with costs of the services divided among the agencies and sub-agencies with staff at the post, based on the level of ICASS services used.

M/PRI has developed standard methodological tools to examine overseas staffing on a mission-by-mission basis. These tools are ratios and formulas that compare missions considered similar in size, foreign policy priority, and management and administrative requirements, and help M/PRI to determine what it believes to be appropriate staffing levels in each section of an overseas post. The total management ratio, for example, is the number of customer units divided by the number of U.S. direct-hire management positions.[14] Further, the level of program staff[15] is analyzed using two tools—the Four Factor Index and diplomatic density. The Four Factor Index is an attempt to measure a country's theoretical

---

[14]The total management ratio is a way to quantify the workload of service providers in the management section by measuring the amount of customer units served. Customer units represent the different customers served by the management section, including U.S. direct-hire staff, their family members, and locally-employed staff.

[15]Program staff include State Department staff in the offices of the chief of mission, political affairs, economic affairs, and public diplomacy.

foreign policy importance to the United States using a combination of factors such as population, gross domestic product, trade volume with the United States, and U.S. foreign assistance. Diplomatic density is an effort to quantify the size of the U.S. diplomatic presence in a country with respect to U.S. interests in that particular country. It is calculated by dividing the number of diplomatic direct-hire positions present in a given country by the Four Factor Index. According to M/PRI officials, diplomatic density tends to be relatively low in developed countries with which the United States has close relations, such as Canada, Japan, and Germany, or where our interests are limited or primarily humanitarian. Diplomatic density may be higher where the United States has or has recently had difficult relations or where vital security interests are at stake, such as in Russia and many of the countries in the Middle East.

Many post officials we spoke with considered M/PRI's standardized analysis appropriate but emphasized the need for flexibility to account for varying circumstances at each post. Some officials noted that M/PRI's comparative analysis among posts was particularly helpful in providing context for staffing decisions. For example, one management officer stated that the rightsizing review found that locally-employed staff at post had heavier workloads than their counterparts at similar posts. The post used this analysis as justification for requesting more locally-employed staff positions.

According to non-State officials, M/PRI generally coordinates with other agencies in preparing rightsizing reviews of U.S. government staffing overseas. In 2006, we reported that coordination with other agencies in the rightsizing process was initially limited.[16] Non-State agencies had voiced a number of concerns regarding their interaction with the Office of Rightsizing, including their desire for greater participation in the rightsizing process. We recommended that the Office of Rightsizing increase its outreach activities with non-State agencies so that all relevant agencies with an overseas presence could discuss rightsizing initiatives on a regular and continuous basis. During our current review, non-State officials stated that M/PRI's current coordination efforts had improved.

---

[16] GAO-06-737.

Over Half of Staffing Projections Were within 10 Percent of Actual Staffing Levels as of December 2011, but Some Posts Have Larger Differences

For more than half of the 144 staffing projections based on rightsizing reviews that we analyzed, actual staffing levels as of December 2011 were within 10 percent of review staffing projections, either higher or lower.[17] However, over 40 percent of the projections based on the reviews had differences of greater than 10 percent. About 30 percent of these had more staff than projected and 13 percent had fewer (see fig. 1). In a few cases, the actual staffing levels as of December 2011 were much higher or lower than the projected levels. For example, the actual number of U.S. direct-hire desk positions (81) in Bolivia as of 2011 was less than half of the projected number of U.S. direct-hire desk positions (164). On the other hand, the actual number of U.S. direct-hire desk positions in Algeria (56) was nearly 20 percent higher than the projected level (45). See appendix I for more information about our methodology.

---

[17]Rightsizing reviews usually project staffing levels 4 to 5 years into the future based on the existing levels at the time of the review. For actual staffing levels, we used data as of December 2011 from State's post personnel database, which includes overseas staff numbers for all agencies. For the projected staffing levels, we used the rightsizing reviews' numbers if the projection year was 2011 and we extrapolated the staffing levels if the projection year was beyond 2011. We did not include all of the rightsizing reviews in the comparison between the actual and projected staffing levels for various methodological reasons, such as data reliability concerns and review time frames that were outside the scope of our analysis. See appendix I for more information about our methodology.

Figure 1: Percentage of Rightsizing Reviews with December 2011 Staffing Levels Over and Under Rightsizing Projections

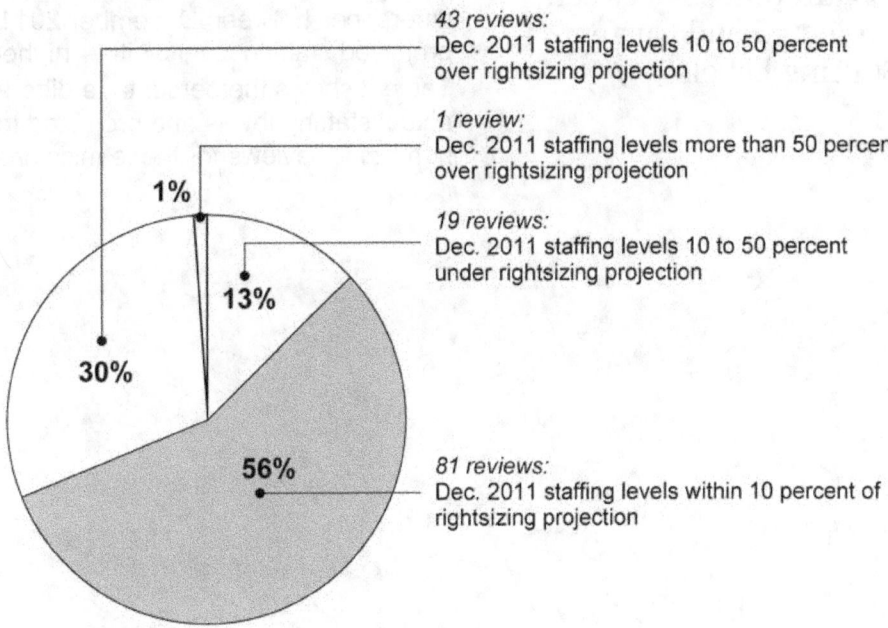

43 reviews:
Dec. 2011 staffing levels 10 to 50 percent over rightsizing projection

1 review:
Dec. 2011 staffing levels more than 50 percent over rightsizing projection

19 reviews:
Dec. 2011 staffing levels 10 to 50 percent under rightsizing projection

81 reviews:
Dec. 2011 staffing levels within 10 percent of rightsizing projection

Source: GAO analysis of rightsizing review reports and State personnel database.

Notes:

1. The projected staffing levels were from the rightsizing reviews if the projection year was 2011 and were extrapolated if the projection year was beyond 2011. The actual staffing levels refer to the levels from the State post personnel database as of December 2011. The database includes overseas staff from State and non-State agencies.

2. Our comparison included 144 rightsizing reviews. We excluded reviews for a variety of reasons, including the following: (1) the projection year was before 2011; (2) the actual staffing level as of December 2011 was deemed unreliable; (3) the review was for an individual post, not for all posts in a country; and (4) the review had no projected staffing level.

Unanticipated Events and Other Factors Contribute to Differences between Projected and Current Staffing Levels

Numerous factors contribute to differences between projected and current staffing levels, such as unanticipated U.S. and foreign government policy changes. Officials from ten missions we identified as having the largest differences between December 2011 staffing levels and the rightsizing projected staffing levels, either higher or lower, identified such factors.[18] Table 2 shows the percentage differences between December 2011 actual staffing levels and projected total staffing levels based on the rightsizing reviews for these missions.

---

[18]To understand the factors that could explain the differences between the actual and projected staffing levels, we identified posts with relatively large differences by generating a composite index for each country. Based on the composite index, we identified the top 5 countries with projected staff levels that were higher than actual levels and the top 5 countries with projected staff levels that were lower than the actual level. We sent questions to the management officers in each of the 10 countries asking for their views on causes for the differences, and received responses from all of them. The following section summarizes responses from the management officers in these countries, as well as Kuwait, a country we visited.

Table 2: Countries with the Largest Differences between December 2011 Staffing Levels and Rightsizing Review Projections

Country	Percentage Differences between December 2011 Total Staffing Levels and Rightsizing Review Projections
December 2011 Staffing Level Below Rightsizing Projection	
Libya	-39
Philippines[a]	-32
Korea	-30
Bolivia	-28
Tunisia	-24
December 2011 Staffing Level Above Rightsizing Projection	
Burkina Faso	30
Mozambique	25
Bangladesh	22
Pakistan	21
Ghana	20

Source: GAO.

Notes:

Because size of missions varies greatly, similar differences in percentages represent a higher number of staff in a larger mission than in a smaller mission.

[a]The management officer in the Philippines explained that the large difference between the projected and the actual staffing levels was because rightsizing projections included certain contractor positions, such as local guards, janitors, gardeners and cafeteria workers that were not included in State's post personnel database, which was the basis for the actual staffing level. After taking out these positions from the projection, the total actual staffing level was close to the projected level. This post was the only location we interviewed where staffing level differences were identified as a result of data differences, rather than other factors related to U.S. operations in the country.

Unanticipated changes in U.S. government policies and priorities contribute to differences between actual and projected staffing levels at overseas posts.[19] Programs such as the President's Emergency Plan for AIDS Relief (PEPFAR)[20] and USAID and State hiring initiatives, including

---

[19]Multiple factors can contribute to the differences between actual and projected staffing levels. The data we have are not at a level of specificity that would allow us to isolate the effect of each of the factors.

[20]PEPFAR is a U.S. government initiative which began in 2008 with the goal to combat HIV/AIDS around the world.

Diplomacy 3.0,[21] have added additional staff to overseas posts, while other changes in U.S. foreign policy have led to lower-than-projected staffing levels.

- According to the management officer in Mozambique, the increase in the number of U.S. direct-hire and locally-employed staff positions as a result of PEPFAR's initiation was greater than anticipated.
- The introduction of the Visa Waiver Program for Korea reduced the need for consular officers to conduct visa interviews and led to lower-than-projected staffing levels, according to the management officer in Korea.
- Ghana became a USAID priority country and the beneficiary of the Global Health Initiative, Feed the Future, and Partnership for Growth, which led to increased staffing levels, according to the management officer in Ghana.
- USAID's and State's hiring initiatives added a human resource officer, a political officer, and a general service officer, positions not anticipated at the time of the rightsizing review, according to the management officer in Mozambique.
- According to the management officer in Pakistan, increased funding to address development and security projects has led to higher staffing levels than the rightsizing review projected.
- The closure of an Arabic language school for State employees in Tunisia resulted in staffing levels below rightsizing projections, according to the management officer.

Unanticipated changes in foreign government priorities and political environment can contribute to differences between actual and projected staffing levels. A foreign government's decision to eliminate program funding or request the closure of a U.S. program usually leads to lower staffing levels, as in the following examples.

- According to the Deputy Chief of Mission in Kuwait, the decrease in Kuwaiti government funding for the Office of Military Cooperation-Kuwait caused the post to reduce staffing levels beginning in 2009.
- In 2008, the Bolivian government ordered the U.S. Drug Enforcement Agency to leave Bolivia, leading to an unexpected reduction in staff, according to the management officer in Bolivia.

---

[21]Diplomacy 3.0 is State's multi-year hiring program to increase its Foreign Service and Civil Service personnel.

- According to the management officer in Libya, staff levels decreased after the evacuation and destruction of the U.S. embassy in February 2011.

Additionally, some posts reported that they were unable to carry out the relatively large reductions in staffing levels projected in the rightsizing reviews, usually for locally-employed staff positions. M/PRI projected sizeable reductions in locally-employed staffing levels for posts through outsourcing or contracting. However, some posts reported that a lack of viable service options in the local economy made it unfeasible to outsource or contract services. For example,

- In Mozambique, outsourcing services such as the motor pool, customs shipping, travel services, and warehousing are not feasible due to the country's poor infrastructure, according to a management officer in the country.
- In Bangladesh, according to a management officer in the country, the post does not contract custodial services, warehouse services, or car repair as recommended by the rightsizing review because no local contracting options exist.
- In Burkina Faso, the embassy did not contract guard services because no major contractors exist in the capital, Ouagadougou, and local companies cannot provide the level of quality and service required by the post, according to the embassy's management officer.

Rightsizing Recommendations Focus on State Administrative and Management Staff, and State Relies on Non-State Agencies to Determine Their Own Staffing Needs

Rightsizing recommendations often focus on administrative or management positions, where efficiencies are considered likely to be achieved. M/PRI typically does not make recommendations to non-State agencies and generally relies on non-State agencies, as well as certain State bureaus, to determine their own staffing needs.

State's Recommendations Generally Focus on State Administrative and Management Staff at a Specific Post to Improve Efficiency

Rightsizing reviews contain recommendations to improve post operations and eliminate duplicative services and positions;[22] these recommendations often focus on State's administrative and management staff. To develop its recommendations, M/PRI reviews the levels of all staff at missions and seeks input from both State and non-State agencies. Many of M/PRI's recommendations that we analyzed focused on State administrative and management staff rather than programmatic staff or staff from other agencies. Officials stated that administrative and management functions are where greater efficiencies are considered likely to be achieved. M/PRI recommendations may include outsourcing or regionalization of administrative functions such as voucher processing or warehousing. These changes affect administrative staff responsible for those functions, at times addressing dozens of positions filled by locally-employed staff. In Albania, for example, the rightsizing review recommended a reduction of over half of the locally-employed staff non-desk[23] positions, from 216 to 93, mainly through outsourcing of guard services. In Bangladesh, the rightsizing review recommended eliminating 27 locally-employed non-desk staff positions out of a total of 192 to improve the efficiency of administrative functions, such as building, gardening, and custodial services. The review found that the number of square meters maintained per service provider for both residential and non-residential buildings in Bangladesh was lower than the worldwide median. For example, the review found that the area a service provider maintained in Bangladesh was less than half that in other posts for non-residential buildings and thus deemed the service to be inefficient. It recommended eliminating a sufficient number of positions to bring the ratio of square meters per service provider on par with other posts.

According to State officials, the focus on management services is appropriate because that is where duplication of effort is most likely to occur. State officials said that it is easier to apply M/PRI's quantitative tools to administrative and management staff activities than to programmatic activities. According to State officials, administrative or management work is better suited to measurements that can be

---

[22]M/PRI officials stated that their recommendations can make posts' administrative services platform more efficient, which can lower costs for all agencies at a post.

[23]Desk positions are those that require the use of designated office and desk space, while those that do not need an office, such as guards and garden and custodial staff, are considered non-desk positions. These designations help OBO determine how much space is needed when planning construction of an embassy or consulate.

compared across posts. For example, voucher examiners can record the volume of vouchers handled in a given time and the length of time they take to process. M/PRI has developed tools to assess the level of administrative support needed at posts of different sizes and has used those tools to compare posts of similar size. By comparing the efficiency of administrative services across similar posts, M/PRI has developed targets that posts should meet and uses these targets to identify posts that may be under- or overstaffed in administrative functions. For example, the rightsizing review for Paraguay recommended that the embassy cut one U.S. direct-hire position in administrative services support, a general services officer. This recommendation was based on comparing the workload of Paraguay's service providers with workloads of service providers at similar posts—Uruguay, Croatia, and Cyprus. Rightsizing reviews also evaluate whether posts can utilize locally-employed staff in a position rather than a more costly U.S. direct hire. For example, the 2010 rightsizing review for Kenya recommended that the post use appointment-eligible family members[24] to serve in office management positions instead of U.S. direct hires. According to M/PRI, the cost of employing these appointment-eligible family members is only a fraction of U.S. direct-hire employees and helps minimize the American footprint in dangerous overseas environments. In addition, M/PRI recommended that appointment-eligible family members be considered for employment if host country nationals are unavailable or present an unacceptable risk.

According to State officials, it is more difficult to quantify the workload of program staff such as political officers than that of administrative and management staff. M/PRI has developed methodological tools to measure a post's diplomatic density and foreign policy priority for comparison with similar posts. However, State officials said that it is difficult to assess the efficiency of program staff due to the qualitative nature of their activities, such as discussing policy issues with their diplomatic counterparts or drafting briefing documents for visiting officials. Nevertheless, M/PRI makes recommendations regarding programmatic staff where possible. In Kuwait, for example, the 2010 rightsizing review

---

[24]An appointment-eligible family member is a U.S. citizen spouse or domestic partner, or U.S. citizen child who is at least 18 and up to their 21st birthday, and who is included on the travel orders of a foreign service or civil service employee or uniformed service member permanently assigned to an overseas post under chief of mission authority. The appointment-eligible family member must be a resident at the employee's overseas post.

recommended the periodic reevaluation of the political and economic sections to assess the possibility of combining them. In some cases, M/PRI has made broader recommendations for posts to review levels of staff across an entire region. For example, M/PRI recommended that the Bureau of European and Eurasian Affairs reevaluate an appropriate presence in former Warsaw Pact country posts, given that the political and economic environment in these countries has shifted dramatically during the past 2 decades.

State Does Not Often Make Recommendations Directed at Other U.S. Government Agencies and Relies on These Agencies to Determine Their Own Staffing Needs Overseas

M/PRI reviews all U.S. government staffing overseas and incorporates staffing data and projections from non-State agencies with a presence overseas.[25] While chiefs of mission have final decision-making authority on staffing changes at their missions, M/PRI officials stated that their office does not have the authority to direct non-State agencies' overseas staffing decisions. M/PRI generally does not analyze staffing numbers of other U.S. agencies overseas or make recommendations affecting these staff. Instead, M/PRI officials stated that they rely on these agencies to conduct their own rightsizing assessments and determine independently what their staffing needs will be for each post. M/PRI infrequently makes recommendations to other agencies, such as USAID. For example, M/PRI recommended that USAID evaluate the distribution of its staff in Central America, questioning the sustainability and cost-effectiveness of high USAID staffing levels in El Salvador and suggesting that USAID's development resources could be better utilized elsewhere in Central America. However, such broader recommendations are an exception in rightsizing reviews and not a common occurrence, according to M/PRI officials.

According to some bureau officials, non-State agencies that are relatively new to operating overseas have been slow to acclimate to the rightsizing process. State officials noted that non-State agency officials in Washington might have a different view of long-range overseas staffing needs than their agency officials at post. Several officials from different regional bureaus said that agencies prefer to conduct their own strategic planning and staffing exercises and view rightsizing as an activity internal to State. Officials from several non-State agencies confirmed that they

---

[25]State's Bureau of Consular Affairs and Bureau of Diplomatic Security also have methodologies for determining staffing levels.

conduct their own internal staffing analyses. For example, officials from the Department of Homeland Security noted that they review overseas staffing on an ongoing basis, since current events dictate the department's operational needs. Similarly, officials from the Centers for Disease Control and Prevention stated that they evaluate overseas staffing through annual updates to their strategic staffing plan and look for opportunities to reduce U.S. direct hires by empowering locally-employed staff to serve in senior management and leadership positions. The Defense Intelligence Agency coordinates the DOD's rightsizing efforts at U.S. posts; DOD components reevaluate positions worldwide as requirements change to ensure that staff are best positioned to achieve the department's mission, according to an agency official.

State Offices Vary in Their Use of Rightsizing Reviews, and State Does Not Monitor Implementation of Rightsizing Recommendations

State uses rightsizing reviews to plan facilities construction and for certain staffing considerations, but some U.S. officials said that use of the reviews is limited, and State officials do not monitor whether recommendations are implemented. State's Bureau of Overseas Buildings Operations (OBO) uses the staffing projections in rightsizing reviews to plan the size and estimate the initial costs of new embassy and consulate compounds. Further, M/PRI uses rightsizing reviews when it assesses requests from State or other agencies to add staff to overseas posts, although the respective chief of mission makes the final decision for his or her mission. However, some regional bureau officials said that they do not actively use the reviews except as a historical overview of staffing, and some post officials said that they do not use the reviews at all. In addition, State often uses documents other than rightsizing reviews to inform decisions in areas such as determining staffing levels and regionalization. Finally, State does not monitor the implementation of rightsizing review recommendations and has not designated an office with that responsibility, making it difficult to know the extent to which rightsizing reviews are having an impact.

Some State Officials Use Rightsizing Reviews to Plan Construction and for Certain Staffing Considerations

State uses rightsizing reviews for various purposes, according to U.S. officials. These officials use reviews to, among other things, plan new construction, assess requests to add staff to a post, and sometimes, in conjunction with other information, allocate resources. In addition, some State officials stated that rightsizing is the only comprehensive process to verify the number of overseas positions and the personnel occupying them.

The reviews that precede the construction of a new diplomatic compound have the most impact, according to M/PRI's fiscal year 2010 report to Congress, because OBO uses the rightsizing projections to plan the size and estimate the preliminary costs of such projects. OBO officials told us that using rightsizing reviews to plan new construction is a significant improvement over the process previously used, which was informal and not systematic.[26] Rightsizing reviews must accompany any proposal for new construction that is sent to the Office of Management and Budget and to Congress. While OBO bases its construction plans on M/PRI's rightsizing review, OBO officials stated that they also verify the staffing numbers in the rightsizing reviews with the staffing numbers in personnel databases and with agency and post officials. If post staffing levels increase by more than 10 percent (the amount of growth space OBO builds in) after a project has started, OBO asks M/PRI to do a rightsizing revision to obtain more accurate numbers and improve construction planning, according to OBO officials.[27] Regional bureau officials stated that they and post officials pay particularly close attention to rightsizing reviews that are conducted in preparation for construction because they want to ensure that OBO plans enough space for the new diplomatic compounds.[28]

Further, M/PRI and post officials stated that they use rightsizing reviews when assessing requests by State or other agencies through the NSDD-38 process to add staff to overseas posts, although the final decision on requests is made by the chief of mission. An M/PRI official stated that rightsizing reviews are intended to be used by the chief of mission to inform decisions on staffing, including those made through the NSDD-38 process. A few post management officers told us that the rightsizing

---

[26]In 2003, prior to the establishment of M/PRI, we reported that U.S. agencies' staffing projections for new embassy compounds were developed without a systematic approach or comprehensive rightsizing analyses. See GAO-03-411.

[27]While many of the new U.S. facilities were planned or built prior to the start of the current rightsizing process, which began in 2004, some were planned using current rightsizing reviews. M/PRI identified 21 rightsizing reviews that were used to plan construction. OBO officials said that most of the new facilities OBO has built have had more staff move in than originally planned. In a 2010 report on new embassy compounds completed between 2001 and 2009, we found that actual staffing levels exceeded the originally-built office space by more than 10 percent at almost half of the new buildings that we analyzed. See GAO-10-689.

[28]According to officials, OBO's planning process typically incorporates a 10 percent future growth allowance to accommodate future unanticipated growth.

process had prompted posts to review staffing requests more carefully. One management officer said that the rightsizing process also prompted a more substantial justification for NSDD-38 requests, adding organization and structure to the decision-making process. Another management officer said that rightsizing prompted the post to launch a new internal mechanism to control growth. The post instituted an internal pre-NSDD-38 vetting process requiring each office or agency to justify the need for a requested position via internal memorandum and explain how it would be funded and address other logistical needs (such as available office space).

In addition, some officials from State bureaus and posts told us that they use rightsizing reviews in a variety of other ways. Bureau of Diplomatic Security officials said that they use rightsizing reviews in conjunction with Office of Inspector General (OIG) reports, annual Mission Strategic Resource Plans (MSRP),[29] and other information to make resource allocation decisions in their annual staffing planning exercise. In addition, an official in Kuwait said that she read the rightsizing review when she arrived at post because it gave a more concise summary of conditions at post than other documents, such as the MSRP. Further, a regional bureau official stated that the primary value of rightsizing was that it forces missions to systematically collect information and plan for future staffing. Several officials stated that undertaking the rightsizing process acts as a check on growth in overseas staffing levels. For example, M/PRI's fiscal year 2011 report to Congress states that M/PRI projected 42 fewer U.S. direct-hire positions than missions had projected.

Some post officials, particularly those in management functions, said that they refer to rightsizing reviews to support staffing changes. For example, the management officer in Paraguay stated that the post concurred with the rightsizing recommendation to eliminate an assistant general services officer position; post officials are now in the process of abolishing the position. The financial management officer in Sarajevo said that she had already considered outsourcing cashiering, but a rightsizing recommendation to do so gave her more incentive to take action. Further, according to M/PRI officials, M/PRI's 2007 review on Uruguay

---

[29]Posts articulate country goals and make budget requests to support those goals through the MSRP. The MSRP serves as the programmatic planning tool for all U.S. government agencies with programming in that country. State is currently in the process of transitioning to a new planning system to replace the MSRP.

recommended adding a second U.S. direct-hire public diplomacy position, and the post has since implemented that recommendation.

According to State officials, M/PRI provides a broader perspective in analyzing overseas staffing, providing information on where posts are overstaffed or understaffed, and recommending potential ways to achieve greater efficiencies. OBO officials stated that rightsizing is an independent process that provides staffing projections. According to regional bureau officials, the rightsizing review is currently the only tool that provides a comprehensive process to verify the number of overseas positions and the personnel occupying them. Officials from several regional bureaus said that M/PRI's broader perspective in analyzing post operations was a benefit to rightsizing, as posts tend to have a narrower, more parochial perspective on what staffing levels are necessary.

Some U.S. Officials Use Rightsizing Reviews Less Often than Other Documents that Are More Timely and More Widely Known

Several U.S. officials stated that they do not actively use rightsizing reviews; they view other documents and tools as more timely and useful for planning and staffing decisions. For example, officials from a regional bureau said that they do not actively use the reviews except as a historical overview of staffing. Officials from one regional bureau said that the 5-year reviews do not have as clear a use as those done specifically for construction. Some State post officials, especially in non-management functions, said that the rightsizing reviews were of little or no use to them.

Several U.S. officials stated that that they use MSRPs and OIG reports more frequently than rightsizing reviews to make staffing and resource allocation decisions. These officials said that they were more aware of the annual MSRPs, which are more current than 5-year rightsizing reviews, and OIG reports and recommendations, which require follow-up until they are closed. Officials said that rightsizing reviews, done every 5 years, quickly become outdated as the situation at a post changes. Officials from the Centers for Disease Control and Prevention said that, while the rightsizing review is a long-term planning document, the more immediate time frame of the annual MSRP is more actionable, given the short-term program-driven nature of the agency's work. Further, some State officials told us that because the rightsizing process is still relatively new and done at each post only once every 5 years, many post management officers have not yet gone through a rightsizing review and may be unfamiliar with it. As a result, some post officials may be resisting the rightsizing process rather than viewing it as a tool, according to M/PRI officials.

In addition, some officials said that the final rightsizing reviews are not widely disseminated, or that they do not know how to find the reviews. Department of Homeland Security officials said that this is the first year State has given them access to the final rightsizing review on State's intranet. Previously, while they provided comments on drafts, they were not given access to the final document. In addition, a human resources officer at one of the posts we visited stated that the training State provides to new human resources officers does not mention the rightsizing review. Several officials at the posts we visited said that they first learned about their post's rightsizing review in an announcement of our visit to discuss rightsizing.

State Does Not Monitor Implementation of Rightsizing Recommendations and Has Not Clearly Designated an Office Responsible for Following Up on Recommendations

State has not clearly designated an office with responsibility for pursuing implementation of rightsizing recommendations and does not track recommendation status after completing a rightsizing review, making it difficult for M/PRI to assess impact.[30] The legislation that established the rightsizing process states that the Secretary of State shall take actions to carry out the recommendations made in each rightsizing review.

State officials have differing opinions about who should be responsible for implementing recommendations. M/PRI's 2010 report to Congress states that rightsizing decisions are implemented through the NSDD-38 process, with the final decision resting with the chief of mission. However, one post official stated that regional bureaus should have responsibility for taking action on rightsizing recommendations because they make resource allocations across posts. Other post and regional bureau officials, in contrast, stated that individual posts have responsibility to take action on rightsizing recommendations because the recommendations are generally directed at the posts, not the bureau. Still other officials stated that the posts and regional bureaus should share responsibility for implementing the recommendations. Officials from one regional bureau said that M/PRI's recent rightsizing recommendations were often developed in concert with the regional bureaus, which could prompt the

---

[30]According to GAO's standards for internal control in the federal government, management should assess the quality of performance over time and ensure that the findings of audits and other reviews are promptly resolved. Resolution could be through correcting identified deficiencies, producing improvements, or demonstrating that the findings and recommendations do not warrant management action. GAO, *Standards for Internal Control in the Federal Government*, GAO/AIMD-00-21.3.1 (Washington, D.C.: November 1999).

bureau to follow up and encourage the post to implement the recommendations. M/PRI began requiring posts to provide recommendation implementation action plans in 2007 in response to one of our previous recommendations.[31] However, officials said that they stopped doing the plans after about a year. The time horizon for implementing the rightsizing recommendations varied to such an extent that frequent reevaluation of progress would have been required to ensure compliance, which was impractical given M/PRI's resource constraints, according to M/PRI officials. Officials from both M/PRI and the regional bureaus have noted that M/PRI does not have the authority to compel implementation of rightsizing recommendations.

Some post officials noted that there is little incentive to implement recommendations, particularly if the recommendations are to decrease the workforce size. While posts may agree with rightsizing recommendations in concept, the tendency is for posts to protect their staffing levels and look for increases if possible. For example, an official in Prague agreed with a rightsizing recommendation to conduct a strategic regional review of staffing in former Warsaw Pact countries to determine whether the number of positions could be reduced. He noted, however, that it would be difficult to accomplish in practice because posts lack incentive to cut positions. The post's budget provides salaries and other compensation for locally-employed staff, while State's headquarters budget provides U.S. direct-hire staff salaries.[32] As a result, posts lack incentive to reduce U.S. direct-hire staff even though they are more costly than locally-employed staff. In addition, the chief of mission in a particular country has final authority over staffing decisions and may have priorities that extend beyond rightsizing considerations.

Because it is unclear which entity is responsible for addressing recommendations, and State does not monitor actions taken in response to rightsizing reviews, State's ability to report to Congress on the results of the reviews is limited. No entity within State monitors implementation of rightsizing recommendations. Some regional bureau officials have stated that, since M/PRI makes the recommendations, it should be M/PRI's responsibility to track their implementation. M/PRI issues an annual report

---

[31]GAO-06-737.

[32]The post budget also provides some benefits to U.S. direct-hire staff.

to Congress[33] in which it lists the rightsizing reviews it has completed, the number of staff positions recommended for elimination, potential cost savings, and information on NSDD-38 decisions to add or abolish positions overseas. M/PRI's fiscal year 2010 report to Congress stated that rightsizing is a tool in reallocating existing personnel resources and related costs and ensuring that requests for new resources are the minimum required to meet national goals and objectives. The report asserted that rightsizing had resulted in 838 fewer U.S. direct-hire positions between 2005 and 2010, decreasing future costs by an estimated $503 million per year for these positions. However, these numbers were simply an accounting of what M/PRI recommended, not what actually occurred. The report did not indicate whether rightsizing review recommendations had been implemented. M/PRI did not review those positions to determine if they were in fact eliminated, and, if so, whether they were reinstated later. In addition, the eliminated positions would not necessarily result in a net cost savings to the government. For example, although some U.S. direct-hire positions might be cut at one post, the persons occupying those positions could then be assigned to a position at a different post. M/PRI officials noted that they no longer calculate decreases in future costs because these numbers are problematic. M/PRI's fiscal year 2011 report to Congress does not include these estimates.

Conclusions

Rightsizing reviews play a crucial role in planning construction of new diplomatic facilities overseas, can inform bureau and post decisions on staffing, and have prompted some posts to reassess staffing increases. M/PRI has improved the consistency of its rightsizing approach over the past several years. In addition, undertaking the rightsizing process can act as a check on growth in overseas staffing. A valuable component of the reviews is the recommendations made to improve post operations.

The legislation that established the rightsizing process requires the Secretary of State to ensure that rightsizing recommendations are addressed; however, State officials have not developed a clear approach or designated an office to address, track, and report on such recommendations. No State office has responsibility for following up on

---

[33]Congress requires State to submit an annual report on the rightsizing reviews that occurred during the previous 12 months, trends in overseas staffing, and the Secretary of State's recommendations regarding such reviews.

recommendations, and posts or bureaus have limited incentive to undertake an examination of recommendations and implement them if they prove to have value. Further, any actions post officials take to implement recommendations may not be known or documented outside the post, which contributes to a substantial loss of information for State officials. Although the reviews have certain limitations, including competing priorities at posts, State has not yet realized the full potential of its rightsizing reviews. To strengthen the impact of future rightsizing reviews, State needs a process by which it can capture this information to inform future decisions about the optimal number and mix of staff at posts overseas to maximize the use of limited resources. Such a process would also strengthen State's ability to report to Congress on the accomplishments of its rightsizing process.

Recommendations for Executive Action

To strengthen the effectiveness of the rightsizing effort, we recommend that the Secretary of State designate the appropriate entity or entities to take the following two actions:

1. ensure that rightsizing recommendations are addressed, including time frames for their evaluation and implementation, and

2. track and report on the actions taken to implement the recommendations.

Agency Comments and Our Evaluation

We provided a draft of this report to State for comment. In its written comments, reproduced in appendix II, State emphasized that correctly aligning staffing with foreign policy goals and ensuring the maximum safety and efficiency of overseas operations remain top department priorities. State also noted that, given the critical role rightsizing reviews play in determining staffing levels in preparation for the construction of diplomatic facilities overseas and informing bureau and post decisions on future staffing needs, it is important that the rightsizing function be carried out optimally and that rightsizing data and analysis be shared widely.

State indicated that it would carefully consider our recommendations, and it described a number of actions it intends to take that could address them. State noted that M/PRI will take the lead with regard to tracking implementation of rightsizing review recommendations. For rightsizing reviews initiated after August 1, 2012, as part of the ongoing second cycle of reviews, M/PRI analysts will outline the extent to which specific recommendations M/PRI provided in the previous rightsizing cycle have been implemented, as appropriate. State proposed that this information on progress related to implementation of M/PRI's recommendations for overseas posts be included in the yearly rightsizing report to Congress beginning in December 2012. In addition, beginning in calendar year 2013, M/PRI will survey each mission 1 year after the completion of a rightsizing review to assess progress with regard to the implementation of recommendations. Posts will be asked to report on measures taken to comply with recommendations, provide a time frame for doing so, or explain changing conditions or policies that make compliance unfeasible. State proposed to then include this additional information in the yearly rightsizing report to Congress beginning in December 2013. Further, State reported ongoing efforts to refine analytical tools used in the rightsizing analysis and cited an intention to expand the number of outreach sessions and training on rightsizing to classes at its Foreign Service Institute.

State also provided technical comments that were incorporated, as appropriate. We provided the Departments of Defense; Health and Human Services; Homeland Security; and Justice; and the U.S. Agency for International Development with relevant excerpts of the report and requested technical comments, but none were provided.

We are sending copies of this report to interested congressional committees. We are also sending copies of this report to the Secretary of State. In addition, this report is available at no charge on the GAO website at http://www.gao.gov.

If you or your staff have any questions about this report, please contact me at (202) 512-8980 or courtsm@gao.gov. Contact points for our Offices of Congressional Relations and Public Affairs may be found on the last page of this report. GAO staff who made key contributions to this reported are listed in appendix III.

Michael J. Courts
Acting Director, International Affairs and Trade

Appendix I: Scope and Methodology

The objectives of this report were to examine (1) the consistency of the Department of State's (State) approach to conducting rightsizing reviews and how its projections compare to actual staffing levels; (2) the focus of State's rightsizing recommendations; and (3) the extent to which State uses its rightsizing reviews and monitors implementation of recommendations.

Our scope included the 181 rightsizing reviews that State's Office of Management Policy, Rightsizing and Innovation (M/PRI) completed between 2005 and 2011 that were provided within the time frame of our review. Each U.S. overseas mission has undergone at least one rightsizing review, according to M/PRI; a few have undergone two reviews.

To obtain information on the consistency of State's approach to conducting rightsizing reviews, the focus of rightsizing recommendations, and the extent to which State uses its rightsizing reviews and monitors implementation of recommendations, we reviewed agency documents—including M/PRI's annual reports to Congress, and Office of Inspector General (OIG) reports—and interviewed officials from State and non-State agencies, both in Washington, D.C., and at overseas posts. Specifically, we discussed rightsizing with State officials in Washington from M/PRI, regional bureaus, the Bureau of Overseas Buildings Operations; the Bureau of Diplomatic Security; the Bureau of Consular Affairs; and the OIG. We also spoke with officials from non-State agencies in the United States and overseas, including the Departments of Commerce, Defense, Health and Human Services, Homeland Security, and Justice, and the U.S. Agency for International Development.

To obtain more detailed information on the consistency of State's approach to conducting rightsizing reviews, how projections compare to actual staffing levels, the focus of rightsizing recommendations, and how State uses and monitors implementation, we selected 14 reviews to analyze in greater depth, traveling to 3 of the posts and contacting the other 11 by telephone or email. We based our selections on interviews with M/PRI and State's regional bureaus, the content of the rightsizing reviews, and the political and security conditions at post to ensure that we analyzed a range of experiences. In selecting posts, we considered the date the rightsizing review was completed, whether other U.S. agencies were present at post, geographic diversity and whether a post was located in a new embassy compound. We traveled to Prague, the Czech Republic; Sarajevo, Bosnia and Herzegovina; and Kuwait City, Kuwait to discuss their respective rightsizing reviews with post officials. While at post, we interviewed officials in each embassy section, including the office of the chief of mission, management, human resources, financial management, facilities management, the regional security office, political affairs, public affairs, and consular affairs, among others. We also met with officials from other U.S. government agencies present at post. We also communicated with management officers at the following 11 missions: Bangladesh, Bolivia, Burkina Faso, Ghana, Korea, Libya, Mozambique, Pakistan, Paraguay, the Philippines, and Tunisia.

To obtain additional information on the consistency of State's approach to conducting rightsizing reviews, we reviewed agency documents—including M/PRI's annual reports to Congress, M/PRI's guidance to posts, and M/PRI's guide to rightsizing for its analysts—and interviewed officials from State and non-State agencies, both in Washington, D.C., and at overseas posts. During our overseas site visits to the Czech Republic, Bosnia and Herzegovina, and Kuwait, we discussed the rightsizing process with the embassy section heads. To examine M/PRI's coordination with other U.S. government agencies, we spoke with officials from non-State agencies in the United States and overseas. We also discussed their process for allocating overseas staff with these officials. In addition, we reviewed legislation related to the establishment of the Office of Rightsizing within State and the intent of rightsizing. To examine how M/PRI's methodology has evolved in recent years, we reviewed 181 rightsizing reviews completed by M/PRI between 2005 and 2011. We reviewed information papers on M/PRI's methodological tools for assessing both administrative staff and program staff, including the total management ratio and diplomatic density.

To assess the extent to which State's staffing projections compare with actual staffing levels, we relied on two main sources of data: (1) the staffing projections in the rightsizing reviews, which we manually entered into a spreadsheet and (2) the actual staffing levels State extracted from the Post Personnel database for us. To assess the reliability of the data, we conducted a data consistency check and interviewed knowledgeable State officials on how the data were collected and maintained, as well as how the data were extracted for our use. We sent the staffing projection data we manually entered to State for verification. We determined that the data were sufficiently reliable for our purpose of comparing staffing projections with actual staff levels as of December 2011. We obtained 181 rightsizing reviews from the Office of Rightsizing. We took the following steps to reduce the number of reviews to 144 for the comparison analysis:

- deleted entries with projection years prior to 2011;
- deleted entries based on an older review if there were multiple reviews;
- deleted entries with unreliable data. For example, State told us that Afghanistan personnel numbers were not reliable;
- consolidated projections for bilateral and multilateral missions in the same country. For example, we combined projections for the U.S. missions to Belgium, the European Union, and the North Atlantic Treaty Organization into one entry;
- consolidated projections for multiple posts in one country into one entry. For example, we consolidated projections for posts in Russia and posts in Poland; and
- deleted entries with no projections.

To compare rightsizing projections to the actual staffing levels of 2011, which is the year for which State provided personnel data, we extrapolated 2011 staffing levels based on rightsizing review projections. We assumed linear growth or decline in staffing levels. For example, if the base year was 2008 and the projection year was 2013, we divided the change in staffing levels by 5 (5 years between the projection year and the base year) to get the annual change in staffing levels. We added the changes for 3 years (3 years between the base year and 2011) to the base-year staffing level. We then identified the number of reviews in each category of differences between the actual and the projection: within 10 percent, 10 to 50 percent overprojection, 10 to 50 percent underprojection, more than 50 percent overprojection, and more than 50 percent underprojection. Missions with overprojections had fewer staff than projected, while those with underprojections had more.

To understand the factors that could lead to differences between the actual and projected staffing levels, we identified posts with relatively large differences by generating a composite index for each country, taking into consideration the differences in absolute numbers and percentages for the following three categories: (a) U.S. direct-hire desk positions, which have the most significant impact on the physical space at a post; (b) locally-employed staff, which comprise the majority of the personnel overseas; and (c) country total, which captures all personnel at a post . Based on the composite index, we identified five countries for overprojection—Tunisia, Libya, Bolivia, Korea, and the Philippines—and five countries for underprojection—Pakistan, Bangladesh, Ghana, Mozambique, and Burkina Faso. The differences between projected and actual total staffing levels as of December 2011 were over 10 percent for all 10 countries. We then sent questions to the management officers in each country asking them the reasons for the differences. We summarized their responses in the report.

To obtain information on the focus of recommendations made by State's rightsizing office, we reviewed 181 rightsizing reviews completed by M/PRI between 2005 and 2011. During our overseas site visits to the Czech Republic, Bosnia and Herzegovina, and Kuwait, we discussed the rightsizing recommendations with the relevant section heads at each post. We also discussed rightsizing recommendations with the management officers in the other 11 missions that we selected for more in-depth review.

To assess the extent to which State uses its rightsizing reviews and tracks implementation of recommendations, we reviewed agency documents, including M/PRI's annual report to Congress, and interviewed officials from State and non-State agencies, both in Washington, D.C., and at overseas posts to obtain information on how officials use the reviews and monitor implementation. In addition, we reviewed our prior work on rightsizing, embassy construction, and guidance on internal controls.

Appendix II: Comments from the Department of State

United States Department of State
Comptroller
1969 Dyess Avenue
Charleston, SC 29405

JUL 0 9 2012

Dr. Loren Yager
Managing Director
International Affairs and Trade
Government Accountability Office
441 G Street, N.W.
Washington, D.C. 20548-0001

Dear Dr. Yager:

We appreciate the opportunity to review your draft report,
"OVERSEAS RIGHTSIZING: State Has Improved the Consistency of Its
Approach, but Does Not Follow up on Its Recommendations" GAO Job
Code 320854.

The enclosed Department of State comments are provided for
incorporation with this letter as an appendix to the final report.

If you have any questions concerning this response, please contact
Margot Carrington, Deputy Director, Office of Management Policy,
Rightsizing and Innovation at (202) 647-6477.

Sincerely,

James L. Millette

cc: GAO – Michael J. Courts
      M – Patrick Kennedy
      State/OIG – Evelyn Klemstine

Department of State Comments on GAO Draft Report

<u>**OVERSEAS RIGHTSIZING: State Has Improved the Consistency of Its
Approach, but Does Not Follow up on Its Recommendations**</u>
(GAO-12-799, GAO Code 320854)

Thank you for allowing the Department of State the opportunity to comment
on the draft report *"Overseas Rightsizing: State Has Improved the Consistency of Its
Approach, but Does not Follow up on Its Recommendations,"* which discusses
progress in the Department's rightsizing efforts.

Correctly aligning staffing with foreign policy goals and ensuring the
maximum safety and efficiency of overseas operations remain top Department
priorities. The GAO report highlights the numerous ways in which the
Department's rightsizing process contributes to these goals. In spite of the fact that
we operate in many high threat environments and in areas of the world undergoing
rapid change, the systematic and analytical framework for making staffing decisions
engendered by rightsizing is now part of the Department's approach to making
resource allocation decisions. As noted in the report's conclusion, rightsizing
reviews play a critical role in determining accurate staffing levels in preparation for
the construction of diplomatic facilities overseas. Moreover, rightsizing can inform
bureau and post decisions on future staffing needs and acts as "a check on growth."
The Department appreciates that GAO found that recommendations geared to
improving post operations through outsourcing, regionalization and the elimination
of duplicative staff and functions were valuable components of the reviews.

Given this valuable role, it is critical that the rightsizing function be carried
out optimally and that rightsizing data and analysis be shared widely. The
Department appreciates GAO's interest in further strengthening our efforts in this
regard and will consider the report's recommendations very carefully.

<u>**Recommendations that State designate the appropriate entity or entities to
ensure that 1) Rightsizing Recommendations are Addressed, Including Time
Frames for their Evaluation and Implementation 2) the Actions Taken to
Implement the Recommendations are Tracked and Reported**</u>

As the GAO report underscored, rightsizing is a process that involves
numerous players in the Department, including the regional and functional
bureaus, overseas missions, and the office of Management Policy, Rightsizing, and

2

Innovation (M/PRI). M/PRI will take the lead with regard to tracking the implementation of recommendations as outlined below.

The Department has completed successfully at least one rightsizing review of every overseas mission and has started the second round of rightsizing. This provides the Department a baseline to assess the extent to which a particular post has followed previous rightsizing recommendations for improving staffing alignment and post operations. For rightsizing reviews initiated after August 1, 2012, M/PRI will outline the extent to which specific recommendations M/PRI provided in the previous rightsizing cycle have been implemented, while taking into account changing conditions and policies that might have made implementation difficult or no longer appropriate. Rightsizing reviews are distributed to overseas missions, regional and functional bureaus in the Department, and the interagency community. Moreover, reviews are also posted by M/PRI on the Department's internal website, ensuring that all information related to implementation of rightsizing recommendations is widely available. The Department proposes that the yearly report to Committees of Congress on "Rightsizing Reviews at Missions Overseas and the NSDD-38 Process," which outlines rightsizing reviews completed during that fiscal year, include information based on these progress assessments, starting with the December 2012 report.

Beginning as soon as is technically feasible in CY 2013, M/PRI will survey each mission one year after the completion of a rightsizing review to assess progress with regard to the implementation of recommendations at this early stage in the five-year rightsizing cycle. Posts will be asked to report on measures taken to comply with recommendations, provide a time frame for doing so, or explain changing conditions or policies that make compliance unfeasible. The Department further proposes to include this additional information in the December 2013 yearly report to Congress.

As some officials at overseas posts told GAO, rightsizing provides a context for staffing decisions and helps support staffing changes. As a management officer at one post explained to GAO, M/PRI's comparative analysis helped form the justification for a request for more locally employed staff positions. At the same time, some regional bureau officials reported to GAO that the broader perspective provided by rightsizing was beneficial, particularly since posts tend to have more "parochial" views about the staffing levels they require. This highlights the extent to which the analysis that M/PRI provides as part of its five year rightsizing reviews can influence the strategic planning process. GAO recognized the improved methodologies and analytical tools that the Rightsizing Office employs

3

in its reviews; M/PRI continues to refine these tools to help us better align staffing resources. For example, the M/PRI Innovation Office just deployed a new interface that displays graphically the efficiency of locally employed ICASS staff, allowing comparisons of management operations at similar posts.

As the GAO notes, chiefs of mission have full authority to determine the composition of staff at their missions. The President instructs chiefs of mission to eliminate duplicative staff and functions, and to bear in mind that rightsizing is an ongoing requirement. Some post management officers shared with GAO the fact that the rightsizing process had prompted their posts to review staffing requests made through the NSDD-38 process more carefully, including in one case demanding "a more substantial justification for NSDD-38 requests", and in another case "launching a new internal mechanism to control growth." M/PRI will further encourage posts to adopt such mechanisms by widely disseminating these types of best practices. Moreover, when NSDD-38 staffing requests are forwarded to posts, M/PRI will continue including comments that incorporate relevant rightsizing analysis to help inform these staffing decisions.

Enhancing our training of management and human resources officers, who play a leading role in rightsizing, provides yet another way for the Department to ensure the maximum effectiveness of the rightsizing process. M/PRI will expand the number of outreach sessions and training on rightsizing to classes at the Department's Foreign Service Institute. At the same time, interagency conferences have been shown to be an effective way to foster coordination and collaboration, and to bring other agencies with an overseas presence up to date on rightsizing initiatives. The Department plans to hold the next interagency rightsizing conference in Washington, D.C., in early FY 2013.

Appendix III: GAO Contacts and Staff Acknowledgments

GAO Contact	Michael J. Courts, (202) 512-8980 or courtsm@gao.gov
Staff Acknowledgments	In addition to the individual named above, Ming Chen, Debbie Chung, Lynn Cothern, Martin de Alteriis, Mark Dowling, Etana Finkler, Leslie Holen (Assistant Director), Heather Latta, Lisa Reijula, and Christina Werth made key contributions to this report.

GAO's Mission	The Government Accountability Office, the audit, evaluation, and investigative arm of Congress, exists to support Congress in meeting its constitutional responsibilities and to help improve the performance and accountability of the federal government for the American people. GAO examines the use of public funds; evaluates federal programs and policies; and provides analyses, recommendations, and other assistance to help Congress make informed oversight, policy, and funding decisions. GAO's commitment to good government is reflected in its core values of accountability, integrity, and reliability.
Obtaining Copies of GAO Reports and Testimony	The fastest and easiest way to obtain copies of GAO documents at no cost is through GAO's website (www.gao.gov). Each weekday afternoon, GAO posts on its website newly released reports, testimony, and correspondence. To have GAO e-mail you a list of newly posted products, go to www.gao.gov and select "E-mail Updates."
Order by Phone	The price of each GAO publication reflects GAO's actual cost of production and distribution and depends on the number of pages in the publication and whether the publication is printed in color or black and white. Pricing and ordering information is posted on GAO's website, http://www.gao.gov/ordering.htm. Place orders by calling (202) 512-6000, toll free (866) 801-7077, or TDD (202) 512-2537. Orders may be paid for using American Express, Discover Card, MasterCard, Visa, check, or money order. Call for additional information.
Connect with GAO	Connect with GAO on Facebook, Flickr, Twitter, and YouTube. Subscribe to our RSS Feeds or E-mail Updates. Listen to our Podcasts. Visit GAO on the web at www.gao.gov.
To Report Fraud, Waste, and Abuse in Federal Programs	Contact: Website: www.gao.gov/fraudnet/fraudnet.htm E-mail: fraudnet@gao.gov Automated answering system: (800) 424-5454 or (202) 512-7470
Congressional Relations	Katherine Siggerud, Managing Director, siggerudk@gao.gov, (202) 512-4400, U.S. Government Accountability Office, 441 G Street NW, Room 7125, Washington, DC 20548
Public Affairs	Chuck Young, Managing Director, youngc1@gao.gov, (202) 512-4800 U.S. Government Accountability Office, 441 G Street NW, Room 7149 Washington, DC 20548

Please Print on Recycled Paper.